The North Worcestershire Path & Midland Link

by John Roberts

*
WALKWAYS

****
WALKWAYS
John Roberts
67 Cliffe Way, Warwick
CV34 5JG   01926 776363
****

THE
NORTH WORCESTERSHIRE PATH
& MIDLAND LINK

by John Roberts

ISBN 0 947708 36 7

First Published 1998

Contents

Why the Midland Link?

The map shows the network of Long Distance Paths in the western Midlands. For clarity I have not shown the *Severn Way* which follows the river, the *Coventry Way* encircling that city, or my own soon to be republished *Birmingham to Aberystwyth Walk* and *Birmingham to Bala Walk*. You can see the connections forged by my Midland Link route- **(6)**.

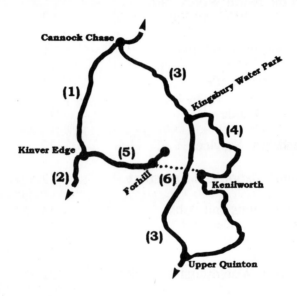

(1) *The Staffordshire Way* - 95 miles between Congleton Edge and Kinver Edge.

(2) *The Worcestershire Way* - 48 miles between Kinver Edge and Holly Bush.

(3) *Heart of England Way* - 100 miles between Cannock Chase and Bourton on the Water.

(4) *Centenary Way* - 100 miles between Kingsbury Water Park and Upper Quinton (both on HoEW).

(5) *North Worcestershire Path* - 27 miles between Kinver Edge and Shirley.

1

Meet the North Worcs Path
.... and the Midland Link

Hereford & Worcestershire County Council established the
North Worcestershire Path in 1983 to link the four Country
Parks to the west and south of Birmingham. The southern part
of Kinver Edge forms their Kingsford Country Park, further
west are the Clent Hills, then the less well known Waseley
Hills and finally the Lickeys.

This simple but brilliant idea was enhanced by a happy acc-
ident. The County Council happened to own a small area of
land in the bend of a road at Forhill, an obscure point south
of the Birmingham suburb of Kings Norton. Probably lacking
any other use for it, they made a picnic site, and so after an
interval the NWP stretched east from the Lickey Hills to
Forhill, making a total length of 21 miles.

There the walk ended for some years, until someone decided
that a short Long Distance Path should not end nowhere in
particular, so they took it north-east from Forhill to Major's
Green on the Solihull boundary and abandoned it by a housing
estate. Major's Green seems hardly more significant a spot
than Forhill. However, the County Council wanted to take
the route to some public transport and they have long term
plans for a Country Park at the abandoned Shirley Quarry.
The countryside on this section is pleasant enough, fields
and hedges and trees, but it has not the quality or the views
of the rest of the NWP and there is more road walking than
it can really sustain.

These public open spaces along the NWP are owned and
managed by several bodies. The larger, northern, portion
of Kinver Edge in Staffordshire has long been in the hands
of the National Trust. So have the Clent Hills and the Chad-
wich Estate on the southern flanks of the Waseley Hills.
Hereford & Worcester County Council own and manage the

2

East from Kinver Edge

Bitell Reservoirs
from Bilberry Hill

N Worcs Path at Iverley

southern part of Kinver Edge and the Waseleys, and until recently managed the Clent Hills. They also have the Forhill site and Shirley Quarry, not yet developed into a park. The Lickeys are owned and managed by the City of Birmingham.

The County Council therefore had a strong interest in most of the important places along the NWP, and as the Highway Authority for all of it, they were responsible for the footpaths. This allowed them to press ahead with creating a Long Distance Path, needing to liaise only with City of Birmingham. But the scheme has fallen down at its eastern end because the County could not look at it as walkers might, and find a worthwhile destination outside their own boundaries.

The **Midland Link** adds this missing dimension to the North Worcestershire Path by giving it a real destination. From Forhill it passes through Wythall, Earlswood Lakes, Tanworth in Arden, Umberslade, Lapworth, Kingswood Canal Junction and Baddesley Clinton before setting off for Kenilworth. It forms a new long distance route linking the Staffordshire Way and Worcestershire Way at Kinver Edge with the Heart of England Way at Baddesley Clinton and the Centenary Way at Kenilworth.

Hills, Views and Villages

The small hills that lie across the south-west corner of the West Midlands area are quite different from one another in shape and character. What they have in common is to be shapely and beautiful and to give two contrasting sets of views. To one side is the urban area of the Black Country and Birmingham, and on the other the deep, quite countryside of Shropshire and Worcestershire.

Kinver Edge is a two mile long sandstone ridge reaching 165 metres in height, it is well wooded and comparatively wild. Although well visited, you will never see so many people here as on the other hills. The views to the west are of the Clee and Abberley Hills and the Wrekin, though they are obscured in many places by intervening ridges.

Leaving the Edge, the NWP falls gently into the valley of the River Stour, then climbs out again over a raised, sandy area of former heathland known as the Iverley Ridge to reach Hagley. Here the path starts to rise again to climb the Clent Hills. These are steep and rounded ice sculptures surfaced with a mean, stony soil known as Clent Breccia, made of 250 million year old sandstone. The lower slopes are wooded, though less densely than Kinver Edge, and the Clents are nobly and proudly bald. Adams Hill to the west at 304 metres gives the widest views - the Wrekin, the Clee Hills, Hay Bluff and the distant Radnor Forest in Wales, the Abberleys and the Malverns. Further south is the broad hump of Breedon Hill and the low ridge of Warwickshire's Edge Hill.

From Adam's Hill the NWP cross a valley to climb Walton Hill at 315 metres. Walton is even more bald than Adam's Hill and presents a steep face to the townscape in the north but a more gentle slope to the south. The NWP follows a long ridge south from Walton Hill which ends at Calcot Hill - 240 metres. This is a magnificent walk across the heads of steep and wooded green ridges and valleys.

A field path leads down the back of a smooth hump of a hill into a narrow, shady valley. From here there are no footpaths, no tracks, and the NWP runs on in the only way possible. It takes to the tarmac for nearly a mile to climb a crippling gradient to the top of Romsley Hill. Dense and mysterious Great Farley Wood sweeps down on either side, mysterious because there is no right of way by which the public can explore it. If there were such a route this part of the NWP might be even steeper.

Romsley Hill is distinguished by a water tower painted in different shades of blue. It is also the point at which the

5

views from the NWP open out. From Kinver Edge to this point, excluding the Clent Hills, views have been occasional or limited. From here until you leave the Lickey Hills, the Abberley Hills and the Malverns are on display, and the great sweep of country towards Bredon Hill.

The NWP now falls sharply into the valley followed by the Bromsgrove - Halesowen road, and meets its only pub not in a village - the Manchester Inn.

It is now only a quarter mile onto the 287 metre Waseley Hills, broad green domes with few trees. The contrast between the placid contours of Wasleys and the dramatic outlines of the Clent and Lickey Hills is due to their geology. The Waseleys are clay.

The Waseley Hills and the Lickeys are virtually continuous, separated only by a bridge over the A38 and a pleasant track. These hills are like the Clents in general character and the tops are surfaced with the Breccia, but their lower slopes have more fertile stuff and are more thickly wooded. The Lickeys are altogether bigger, steeper and grander.

The NWP first climbs Beacon Hill, where you can play mediaevil war games around the mock castle, then plunges down through woods to cross the steep, deep, valley dividing the main hills. The County Council's waymarked route now runs up a dull, wooded valley which has the sole virtue of being easy on the legs. Here I offer a stunning and beautiful alternative up Bilberry Hill. It is beautiful because of huge views, bilberry, heather, birch and pines, and stunning because of the steep climb.

After Bilberry Hill comes a long, slow drop to the Bittell Reservoirs. This section has a couple of fields and a lane and is simply pleasant. But the reservoirs are broad and exciting stretches of water with that feeling of moist air and the watery atmosphere of alders, willows, bog plants, reeds, and the faint splashing of water creatures.

From the reservoirs the path rises through lush green fields to cross the A441, and rises again until it crosses Wast Hill. From the NWP it does not seem much of a hill, but its 210 metres can only be seen from the south where it forms part of a rampart running the next couple of miles to Forhill. This section may seem just a succession of level fields, but the old trees, rich hedges and occasional pond give it a special rural character, and to the south there are surprising views.

Forhill has nothing to show except a radio mast, a pub and the picnic site, but for some reason I have always found it an exceptionally nice place to be.

The rest of the NWP to Major's Green has a couple of interesting features, and in the right places I say a little about the moated farm near Wythall, Berry Mound Fort and Shirley Quarry. The landscape is pretty much the same over this part of the Path, heaving green fields, thick hedges and clusters of trees. In spring time it foams with blossom and twinkles with buttercups, but then, so does everywhere else. Much of the land is under horsi-culture, mind the electric fences. There are no views to speak of.

The Midland Link is a glorious passage through some of the best parts of Warwickshire. From Forhill it follows the NWP for a mile before diverting south round a golf course to pass St Mary's Church, Wythall. From a distance its red brick tower looks like a gaunt, ghastly, gothic ruin, but it is actually intact and this impression is just a feature of the unusual Victorian design.

After a succession of level tracks and fields the Link leaves Worcestershire to enter Clowes Wood, a very varied and beautiful wood, and then passes Earslwood Lakes with the option of a short tour. After more lanes and fields the ground begins to fall from Wood End into the valley of the River Alne, then rises gently to the pretty village of Tanworth in Arden. The long, straight, tree lined track which follows was once a grand carriage drive to Umberslade Hall, and it is followed by a brief episode of parkland Soon you pass under the M40 to meet the obelisk, seen by speeding thousands who will never get a chance to look at it for more than a few seconds.

The walk heads next for Lapworth and its wonderful old church through a well wooded landscape of rolling green fields. It goes on to join the Stratford on Avon Canal for a mile or so to Kingswood, where the Stratford meets the Grand Union Canal. Here the Midland Link joins the Heart of England Way to Baddesley Clinton, where you can see the grey moated manor house and St Michael's church. The transit of Hay Wood follows, said to be one of the surviving fragments of the Forest of Arden but now mainly planted with Scots pine and Cypress. After a mile or so of road walking to Wroxhall, almost the only tarmac on the route, the way to Kenilworth follows field paths which reach out in a near straight line. The castle can't be seen from any distance and adds something of a surprise ending to the walk.

The Country Code

* Enjoy the countryside and respect its life and work
* Guard against all risk of fire
* Fasten all gates
* Keep your dogs under close control
* Keep to public paths across farmland
* Use gates and stiles to cross fences, hedges and walls
* Leave livestock, crops and machinery alone
* Take your litter home
* Help to keep water clean
* Protect wildlife, plants and trees
* Take special care on country roads
* Make no unnecessary noise

Midland Link at Terry's Green

Earlswood Lakes

Baddesley Clinton church

9

Using the Guide

The North Worcestershire Path is an official County Council route and waymarked from end to end with yellow, blue or grey arrows and its pine cone logo. It is so thoroughly done that you will find your way without written directions and will hardly need maps. However, my detailed sketch maps will be helpful in finding your position and in planning walks, especially since I have added notes about facilities at each of the best starting and finishing points.

In complete contrast, the Midland Link is my own invention and there are no special waymarks, so to follow it you will have to use the step by step directions in this guide.

The route directions are quite separate from the description and comment, they are very terse, and set in short, narrow, numbered paragraphs in a clear and open typeface. These and less obvious features have been adopted for Walkways books after much thought. My aim to give information in easily located and remembered blocks of convenient size, bearing in mind that you will be reading on the move.

Distances in *yards* or *miles* are to give you a ROUGH idea how far to walk. You do not need to measure because you will be given something to look out for, such as a stile or gate. So if I say "go .6 mile to the old mill", you will not start to worry if you can't see the old mill, or whatever, after 200 yards. I use yards where I think you will know how far I mean, but few of us know what 600 yards look like, so for longer distances I turn to fractions of a mile.

Distances in *paces* are given to be COUNTED out if you need to. These are infrequent and only for a few yards at a time. Paces vary but you can allow for being tall or short. The reason for all this is that people carry a pace with them but not usually a measuring tape.

I have largely avoided abbreviations but certain phrases recur. You will sometimes see *half R* (or L) meaning a half turn, or about 45 degrees. Therefore *bear R* (or L) means a narrower angle than a half turn, or just tending away from straight ahead. A *road* has a tarmac surface and is usually big enough for a white line down the middle. *Lanes* are tarmaced but smaller and without white lines. *Drives* are like lanes but not public. *Tracks* are wide enough for a four wheeled vehicle and might have an earth, grass or stone surface. A *path* may have any surface, from mud to tarmac, but is only pedestrian width.

The maps are sketches to an approximate scale of 4ins/1 mile (6.3cms/1km). The big black arrow on each map points to north, but you had guessed as much, hadn't you? Small numbers appear on the maps of the Midland Link. These refer to paragraphs in the directions, which have letters and numbers; the westbound route to Forhill - eg **(W33),** and eastbound to Kenilworth Castle - eg **(E41).**

Many people like to carry Ordnance Survey maps and I list the relevant sheets below. You should not need the 1:25,000 scale Pathfinders, but the 1:50,000 Landranger sheets will help you find starting points more easily, and might be useful in case you want to leave the route for an urgent haircut or something.

Landranger Maps (1.50,000) (1.25 ins/mile) (2 cms/km)
    138 Kidderminster & Wyre Forest,
    139 Birmingham,
    140 Leicester & Coventry.

Birmingham 139 covers all but 2.5 miles of both routes.

Pathfinder Maps (1:25,000) (2.5 ins/mile) (4 cms/km)
    933 SO 88/98 Stourbridge & Kinver
    953 SO 87/97 Kidderminster & Bromsgrove
    955 SP 27/37 Solihull & Alvechurch
    955 SP 27/37 Coventry (South) & Kenilworth

Amendment Service

The countryside changes all the time. Paths are diverted and
hedges removed, you will meet new tracks, fences and barns,
To keep walk directions up to date I issue Amendment Slips -
a unique and FREE service.

PHONE ME on 01926 776363 with with a note of the books
that you have and I will send you up to date Slips. EVEN
NEW or recently purchased books can suffer changes within
weeks, it is always worth checking.

PLEASE WRITE OR PHONE to report any changes or
problems stating book, route and paragraph number.

DON'T BOTHER copying changes into your book(s). Just
mark affected paras with highlighter and keep the Slips
in the front of the plastic cover.

Accommodation and Transport

RAIL
There are stations at Hagley, The Lakes (Earlswood Lakes),
Wood End and Kingswood (the station is called Lapworth).
All rail enquiries can be made on 0121 643 2711.

BUSES
The North Worcestershire Wanderer runs on Sundays and
Bank Holidays Mondays to serve many places on the North
Worcestershire Path. It travels in both directions between
Kidderminster via Kinver, Hagley, Clent Hills, Waseley
Hills and Lickey Hills (Rose & Crown) to Barnt Green
Station. You can therefore base your walk entirely on
buses and trains.

Get a timetable with map by phoning the Worcestershire Busline - 0345 125436. In the list of Staring Points etc below I have noted those places served by the Wanderer.

Bus services, frequent and otherwise, do cross the rest of the NWP and the ML and not only at the Starting Points. Services may be altered or stopped so I can only mention where there were services when this was written, and refer you to enquiry lines, which are noted for each place.

CAR
You can motor to any of the Access Points, but at some of them parking space is very limited. If you want to leave more than one car I suggest you check in advance. Pub landlords are often happy for you to park for the day while you walk, but you must ask permission, and it is only reasonable that you sample the pub's offerings.

FEET
To join or leave the NWP from Kinver Village you can use my directions which form the first part of the walk. Note that there is a car park with WCs and picnic tables at the foot of the Edge by a T junction on Sandy Lane.

ACCOMMODATION
These paths are most likely to be walked on day trips by local people, which is just as well because there is hardly any overnight accommodation. However, for those walking these routes as part of a longer treck involving connected LDP's B&B is available on or very near the walks at:

Kinver - enquire on 01384 87756,
Hagley - phone as above,
Nuthurst (symbol between Tanworth and Kingswood)
                                    - 0121 704 6130,
Haseley Knob (just past Wroxall) - 01926 311470,
Kenilworth - 01926 311470.

Starting Points and Pubs

Listed below are the best places to join or leave the NWP and Midland Link, having car parking space or transport connections, pubs etc. I have also listed the very few pubs in between. The western end of the NWP on Kinver Edge is off roads and the nearest facilities are a car park with WCs half a mile away. The best place to start is Kinver village.

On the unwaymarked Midland Link the written route directions start afresh from each Starting Point, and I show the paragraph numbers. Walkers already en route and just passing through may find the wordings at Starting Points a bit odd or superfluous, but they will still be clear. Of course, you can join the routes at any other point, which is easy on the NWP, but on the Link you will have to find the correct paragraph from the map.

North Worcestershire Path

Kinver Village (SO 834846) - Olde White Harte Inn in village off A458 Kidderminster - Bridgnorth road, 4 miles west of Stourbridge. Buses call - phone 0121 200 2700 for routes to or from West Midlands and 01785 223344 elsewhere; NW Wanderer - 0345 125436. Car parks off High Street. The Vine (Free House), Olde White Hart (Hanson's), Plough & Harrow (Batham's), several restaurants, tea shop, Indian take away and chip shop. WCs, chemist, groceries, phones. To reach the start of the NWP on Kinver Edge see first page of directions.

Kinver Edge (SO 829822) - three armed signpost marks meeting of NWP with Worcestershire Way and Staffordshire Way. There is a car park with WCs on route at the foot of the Edge .5 mile away.

Caunsall (SO 850809) - cross roads on A458 Wolver-hampton - Kidderminster road. Buses - 0345 125436. Limited verge parking by canal. Anchor (Free House) and Rock Tavern (Banks's) are .4 mile off A458.

Hagley (SO 913809) - junction of A456 and Bromsgrove Road near Telephone Exchange. Buses - 0121 200 2700; NW Wanderer - 0345 125436. Limited parking in side roads. Spencer's Arms (Banks's), Lyttleton Arms (Big Steak). News and groceries, phone, Porsche dealer.

Clent Hills (SO 939808) - Nimmings Car Park (pay) at Adam's Hill. Buses - NW Wanderer - 0345 125436. Cafe and WCs. To join the NWP follow graded wheelchair route and go up to the summit.

(Pub) Manchester Inn (Free House) on B4551 Broms-grove - Halesowen road. Buses pass - 0121 200 2700.

Waseley Hills (SO 971781) - car park (pay) and Visitor Centre where lane crosses M5. Buses - NW Wanderer - 0345 125436. Cafe, WCs and phone.

Lickey Hills (Rose & Crown) (SO 996759) Old Rose & Crown restaurant on B4096 Rednall - Bromsgrove road. Buses pass - 0121 200 2700; NW Wanderer - 0345 125436. Car park. Cafe and WCs.

Lickey Hills (Visitor Centre) (SO 996759) - at the end of rough track from Lickey church on B4096. Car park. Cafe and WCs.

Forhill (SP 055756) - picnic site off bend of minor road between West Heath and Wythall. Car park with limited opening - check times. The Peacock (Free House). WCs.

Major's Green (SP 101781) - a stile in the fence of Peterbrook Road. Buses - 0121 200 2700. No parking. Trains - Shirley (.5 mile) - 0345 484950. The Draw-bridge (Greenall's) is 400 yards south.

Midland Link

Forhill (E1)- see above.

Earlswood (SP 107734) (E18) (W45) - the gate to "The Lakes" railway station on lane between Earlswood and Terry's Green. Trains - 0345 484950. Buses cross head of lakes - 01926 410410. Car park & picnic site mile on road north from station. No facilities just here. Red Lion (Free House) is .4 mile off route, see sketch map. Phone box by car park.

(Pub) Old Royal Oak (Pubmaster) (SP 108717) Wood End near railway station. Phone nearby.

Tanworth in Arden (SP 113705) (E28) (W36) - war memorial in village 2 miles east of A435. Buses - 01926 410410. Limited parking. Bell Inn (Free House). PO & general store, off licence, phone.

(Pub) Old Royal Oak (Tavern Table) (SP 155714) Nuthurst on A3400, 200yds south of Link.

Kingswood (SP 187709) (E43) (W20) - finger post at canal junction. Buses - 01926 4104100. Trains from "Lapworth" station - 0345 484950. Car park at picnic site by canal. Navigation Inn (M&B). News and general store, off licence. Phone, WCs

Wroxall (SP 225713) (E51) (W12) - bus stop by old Wroxall School on A3400 Birmingham - Warwick road. Buses - 01926 414140. Very limited side road parking. Phone, nursery, cemetery - no other facilities.

Kenilworth (SP 280724) (W1) - car park for castle off B4103 on west of town. All facilities nearby, nearest pubs Queen & Castle Inn (Beefeater) and Clarendon (Courage) on far side of castle.

North Worcestershire Path

Staffordshire Way
Worcestershire Way

Kinver Village
Kinver Edge
Caunsall
Hagley
Clent Hills
Manchester Inn
Waseley Hills
Lickey Hills (Rose & Crown)
Lickey Hills (Visitor Centre)
Major's Green
Forhill
Midland Link

Table of Distances

	kms	miles	Total (miles)
Kinver Village			
Kinver Edge	3.0	1.8	1.8
Caunsall	5.0	3.0	4.8
Hagley	7.0	4.2	9.0
Clent Hills	3.0	1.8	10.8
Waseley Hills	7.0	4.2	15.0
Lickey Hills (R&C)	4.0	2.5	17.5
Lickey Hills (VC)	0.6	0.5	18.0
Forhill	7.3	4.5	22.5
Major's Green	7.3	4.5	27.0

N Worcs Path near Forhill

Forhill			
Earlswood	7.7	4.7	4.7
Tanworth in Arden	5.0	3.0	7.7
Kingswood	9.0	5.5	13.2
Wroxall	5.0	3.0	16.2
Kenilworth	6.3	3.8	20.0

Midland Link

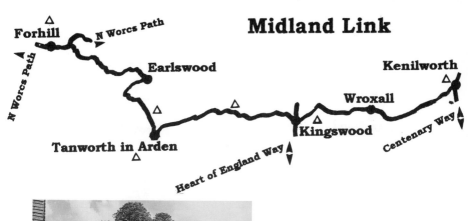

Toombscape at Tanworth in Arden

The North Worcestershire Path & Midland Link

Starting Point	●
Path with bridge	⋅⋅⋅ ►◄ ⋅⋅⋅⋅ ⋅⋅
Track	- - - - - ⌣⌐
Road/lane/drive	⤝
Railway	+++++
Canal	⌣⌣⌣
Stream/river/lake	～～～◯
Woodland	⌒⌒⌒
Hedge/fence	⌐⊤
Church	+
Building	■
Pub	△
Summit	▲

Maps are drawn to an approximate
scale of 4ins/1 mile - 6.3cms/1km

Kinver Village has sprawled a little, as you can see from the north end of Kinver Edge, but with its agreeable High Street of shops, pubs, post office, library, and school, it still has a character and a focus. Most of the buildings are late 19th century or more recent, but there are several from the 18th century and the old grammar school dates from 1511. Kinver's setting in the valley of the winding River Stour is delicious, with the Edge crouched to the south and the river with the Staffordshire & Worcestershire Canal curling round to the east. The village first grew around St Peter's church, perched near the sky on a steep sandstone hill. For centuries its business was farming, and especially wool, but as that declined the village economy became focused on the Stour, which in the 18th and 19th centuries powered five mills producing iron and steel wire. There was also flax production, hatting and glove making. Late in the Victorian era Kinver became popular with Black Country people for Sunday and Bank Holiday visits, and the village began to change its role to that of resort. From 1901 people travelled here from Stourbridge on the Kinver Light Railway, a tram service which local people may wish still existed to reduce village traffic.

Kinver Edge is a mighty sandstone whale of a hill about 1.5 miles long and reaching a height of 166 metres. It falls steeply to the west, but the eastern flank is a gentle slope into the Stour Valley. The Iron Age fort on the crest is the earliest mark of habitation. Cave houses carved from the rosy sandstone were occupied from the Middle Ages and some into the 1950s. During the 1800's twelve families lived in them and later the houses were provided with gas and piped water. The northern part of the Edge owned by the National Trust is managed but natural, with oak and birch over a ground flora of heather, bilberry, gorse and bracken. On the southern part of the Edge there are plantations of Scots pine with some Norway spruce and areas of larch.

Kinver Village to
Kinver Edge

(1) Face Olde White Harte, go R past library & take Vicarage Drive L. At fork go R to gates, then L down fenced path to road.

(2) Go R 200yds to junction by post box. Go L to 30mph sign & turn R up tarmac drive to its end.

(3) Take narrow path L of garage & take small gate. Go ahead 50 paces, then turn R up steep, sandy path. Follow via wooden steps to grassy shoulder. Go L up to crest.

(4) Go L on ridge path 300yds to where grassy spur veers L. Bear R & follow ridge path .75 mile (past trig point) to 3 armed signpost.

Kinver Edge to
Kinver Village

(a) From 3 armed sign post, follow Staffs Way arm along ridge path .9 mile to end of ridge at toposcope.

(b) Go R down steep path to grassy shoulder & wooden fence. Go R down to crossroads of paths in hollow.

(c) Go L & take small gate. Follow path, then drive (round R bend) to lane. Go L to junction by post box.

(d) Go R 200yds to "Church View" L, & just beyond take path L. Follow to track, then go R & join lane to High Street.

21

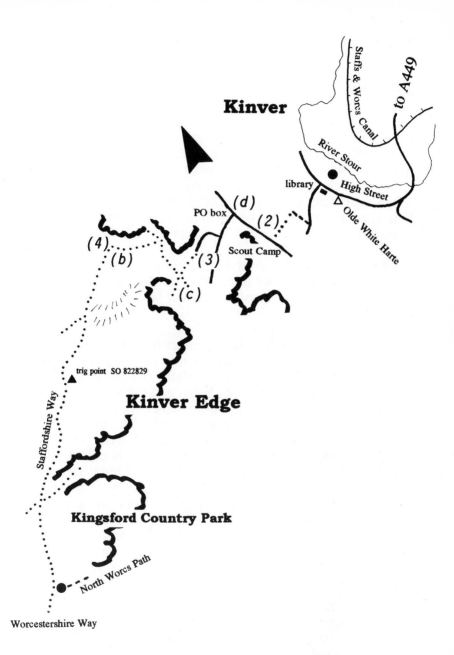

Kinver

Staffs & Worcs Canal

to A449

River Stour

library   High Street

PO box   *(d)*

(2)

Olde White Harte

(4)

(b)   *(3)*   Scout Camp

(c)

trig point   SO 822829

Staffordshire Way

Kinver Edge

Kingsford Country Park

North Worcs Path

Worcestershire Way

The start of the **North Worcestershire Path** is a slight
dip in the ridge with a three armed signpost, a sculptur-
ally twisted oak tree, a roofed display board and picnic
tables. Before leaving, look west. The views are veiled
and mystified by trees, but there is a plunging green
valley and the promise of wonderful things. Invisible
beyond misty ridges are valleys, villages, the River
Severn, the Wyre Forest and the Clee Hills, leading
to the remoteness of south Shropshire and mid Wales.
Kinver and the Edge are western outposts of the huge
urban metropolis to the east. The signpost shows how
how you can explore to the north on the Staffordshire
Way and to the south on the Worcestershire Way.

Leaving the pines of Kinver Edge, you join the first of the
tree lined, sandy, pebbly tracks that are such a feature of
the area. With a few intervals you will be following them
to Hagley.

At Caunsall you cross the **River Stour** by a brick bridge.
Whether it looks just reasonably murky or utterly grey and
dead depends mainly on recent rainfall. The Stour rises on
the northern flank of the Clent Hills, and until it enters the
urban area at Halesowen the water quality is grade C/B
on the Environment Agency's A - F scale. The first letter
shows chemical pollution and the second the biological
state of the water, A being the cleanest. This is only a
rough guide because quality varies daily with temperature
and the amounts of rain and effluent discharges. In the
Agency's 1995 report, the quality of the Stour fell in the
urban area to grade C/E and remained in this state to Lye
where it declined to E/E. At Stourton, just north of Kinver,
the fresher waters of the Smestow Brook help the Stour to
grade D/D, but by the time it reaches the River Severn at
Stourport quality is down again to E/E. There are several
projects in hand to improve the sewage works and restrict
industrial effluent, but rivers are essentially drains and
the only method we have of disposing of our liquid wastes.
You might see the Stour achieve grade C/C in the next few
years, but it will struggle to stay there.

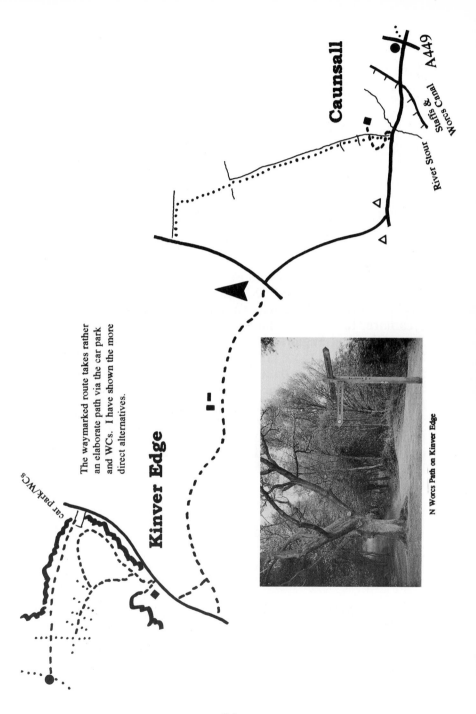

Caunsall

A449

Staffs & Worcs Canal

River Stour

Kinver Edge

car park/WCs

The waymarked route takes rather an elaborate path via the car park and WCs. I have shown the more direct alternatives.

N Worcs Path on Kinver Edge

At Caunsall you also cross the **Staffordshire & Worcester-shire Canal**, winding its 46 miles from Great Haywood on the Trent & Mersey Canal to the River Severn at Stourport. The Shropshire Union and Grand Union Canals have grander embankments and finer viaducts, but the S&W is rivalled only the Stratford on Avon Canal for rural charm. The S&W and the Stratford were both first generation canals, built in 1772 and 1815 respectively. At this time engineering technology and financial markets for raising capital were not well developed, and so construction was made simpler and cheaper by following the contours of the land. Changes of level were kept to a minimum, big tunnels, bridges and embankments avoided, so the early canals ramble happily round the hills.

Most of the NWP from Caunsall to Hagley follows hedged, sandy tracks. They are lined and shaded by trees, usually a mixture of oak, ash, hawthorn, hazel and rather a lot of sycamore. In fact it predominates on the NWP between Fairy Glen and Sugar Loaf Lane. Though introduced by the Romans, sycamore is not a native tree and naturalists regard it as a bit of a pain. It seeds lustfully and the saplings are rampantly successful, it throws deeps shade and tends to oust other species. The objections to "alien" species is not that they have funny accents and don't play cricket, but that not having developed as part of the local environment they offer little habitat for the local bugs and birds. Nor do they suffer from local diseases or predators which might keep them in check.

Hagley is quite a pleasant and convenient place to live, and it does have a rather muted personality. But walking the NWP you meet only the A456, roaring with traffic between Kidderminster, Worcester and Birmingham. Like too many other villages, road traffic has torn Hagley apart.

As you leave Hagley on your way to the Clent Hills you have distant views of **Hagley Hall**. The low bank near to the path is (or was) a haha, or ditch and wall designed to keep farm animals off the lawns but allow views from the house of a landscape uncluttered by fences.

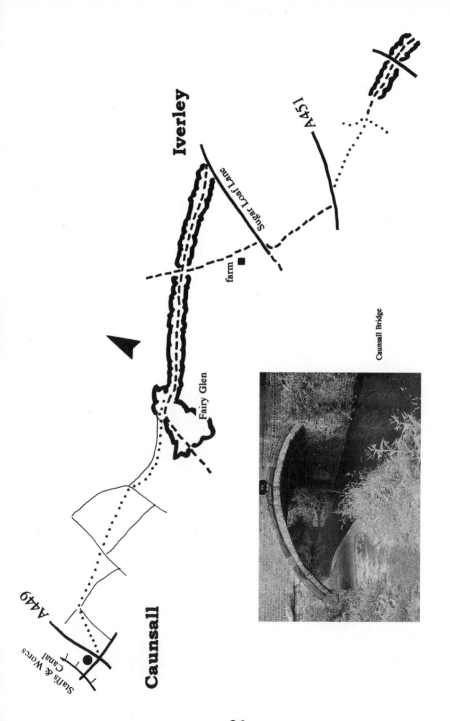

Iverley

Sugar Loaf Lane

A451

farm

Fairy Glen

Caunsall

A449

Staffs & Worcs Canal

Caunsall Bridge

26

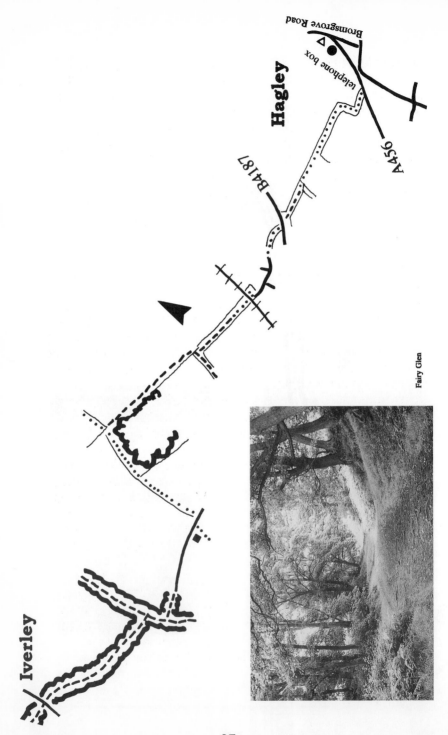

Iverley

B4187

Hagley

Bromsgrove Road

telephone box

A456

Fairy Glen

Hagley Hall has been the home of the Lyttleton family since 1564 but the present house was built in the mid 18th century. The architect was Sanderson Miller who adopted the Palladian style, a pure and stark approach to Greek and Roman architecture which was a reaction to the florid and theatrical Baroque style. There are few local examples of Baroque, but Blenheim Palace in Oxfordshire gives the general idea. There is nothing frivolous about the exterior of Hagley Hall or the other Palladian houses, so it seems curious that they were usually set in romantic, Arcadian landscapes scattered with follies, airy little temples, aimless obelisks and carefully crumbling miniature castles.

There are seven **follies** at Hagley Hall, two of which you can see as you climb the Clent Hills and one which you pass. The totteringly dangerous obelisk still somehow stands on the summit of Wychbury Hill just to the north of Clents. Much closer and below your route to the summit is a shapely mock castle, a copy of a larger version on Edge Hill in Warwickshire. The towers are modelled on those of Warwick Castle. You can't see the Temple of Theseus in the trees below the obelisk, which is little more than an open fronted brick shed with six fluted Doric columns. However, it was the first classical monument in England and the first Greek revival building anywhere. Also out of view is the Prince of Wales's column and an Ionic Rotunda. The folly which you pass is the group of four standing stones on the summit of Adam's Hill. We expect 18th century follies to be grand, imposing, quaint and attractive, so these tedious pieces of rock are a scruffy disappointment. We would be better off with our modern answer to the 18th century folly, garden gnomes.

The **Clent Hills** are eroded outcrops of a 270 million year old coarse sandstone known as Clent Breccia. Past grazing and one million visitors a year have caused serious erosion so that it has broken through the surface in the form of rough gravel. This explains the fences to allow plants to recolonise selected areas.

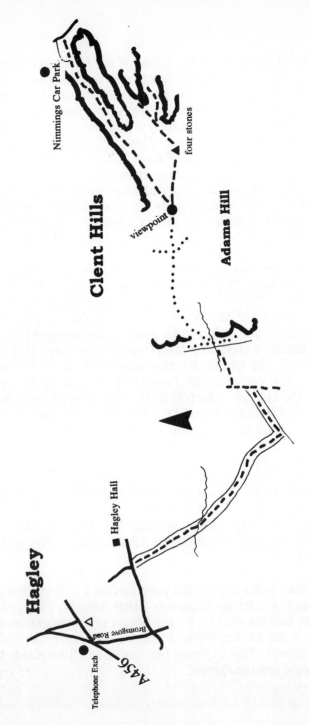

Clent Hills

Nimmings Car Park

four stones

viewpoint

Adams Hill

Hagley

Hagley Hall

Bromsgove Road

A456

Telephone Exch

29

Adam's Hill

Hagley

Walton Hill from Adam's Hill

The Clents are a group of three hills. Your approach from Hagley takes you up the long, steep slope of Adam's Hill at 304 metres, across to Walton Hill at 315 metres and then south to Calcut Hill at 240 metres. Walton Hill is the highest of the three but turns out to be a dome with limited views. Look about instead from the viewpoint on Adam's Hill or from the toposcope on the summit for one of the best views in the Midlands. On a clear day you can see the Wrekin, the Clee Hills, the Radnor Forest in Wales, Hay Bluff, the Black Mountains, the Abberley Hills and the craggy looking Malverns. To the south is the vast, low hump of Bredon Hill and further left, the low ridge of Edge Hill in Warwickshire.

You have probably heard the one about the **Urals**. Going east there is no higher land than this until you reach these mountains in central Russia, and they barely reach 1000 metres.

From **Walton Hill to Calcot Hill** you follow a path just below the crest of a ridge. Above you there is nothing much but a hedge, but to the east the ground falls sharply in a series of green folds into the deep, wooded valley of the Belne Brook. Near the path groups of young trees have been planted, including oak, wild cherry, birch, field maple and beech. Across the valley is the broad flank of Romsley Hill. In the early 1980s Severn Trent wanted to flood it to create a reservoir, an idea that requires no comment.

From Calcot Hill, which is no more than the end point of the ridge, the NWP drops into this valley at **Shut Mill**. This was one of five corn mills powered by the brook; numerous others made edged tools, notably scythes.

The less said the better about the grinding ascent up the lane through **Great Farley Wood** to the top of Romsley Hill. Note that the trees fall away on either side, so you are following the easiest route up a rising ridge. The wood seems to be planted mainly with larch and Norway spruce with some oak on the upper slopes. Deep inside is some terrible secret. This must be so, or why would they girdle the boundaries with barbed wire and post notices shouting "Keep Out". Or is there perhaps no special reason to keep us out?

As you descend Romsley Hill look west for your first views since Adam's Hill of the Abberleys, the Malverns, Bredon Hill and Edge Hill. These will stay with you until you cross the Lickey Hills. Cross the B4551 (Halesowen - Bromsgrove road), then stop up your ears to cross the M5 and reach the Waseley Hills.

In complete contrast to the steep and broken Clent and Lickey Hills, the **Waseley Hills** are smooth green domes. The broad summit gives views mainly over Birmingham to the north-east. The topscope will tell you what is what, but look out for the high points. The next highest point in that direction is the green mop of trees called Frankley Beeches, then you should see the green dome of the water tower at Hollymoor Hospital and the Telecom tower in the City centre. "Big Joe" is the clock on the massive, Italianate tower of Birmingham University. Easier to spot to the left are the radio masts on the Rowley Hills in the Black Country, and Dudley Castle. If you can't see any of this, it is raining, and you are totally fed up with people going on and on about views.

The Waseley and Lickey Hills are almost continuous and the connection involves hardly any road walking. After crossing the A38 by a bridge you join a pleasant wooded track, then a footpath which brings you to a golf course.

From Adam's Hill

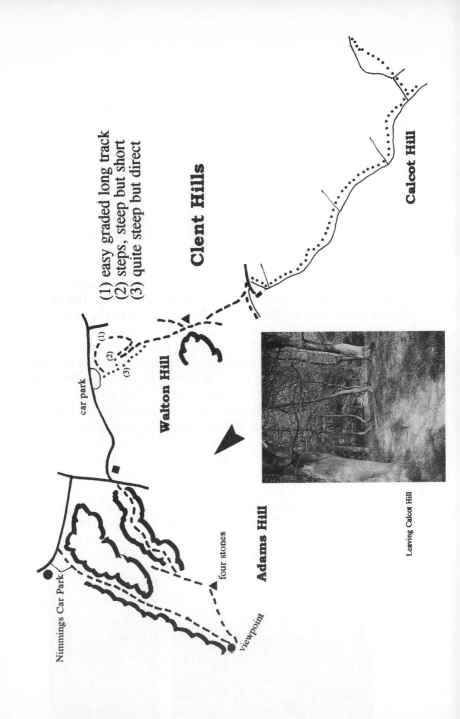

(1) easy graded long track
(2) steps, steep but short
(3) quite steep but direct

Clent Hills

Calcot Hill

car park

(1)
(2)
(3)

Walton Hill

Adams Hill

four stones

viewpoint

Nimmings Car Park

Leaving Calcot Hill

33

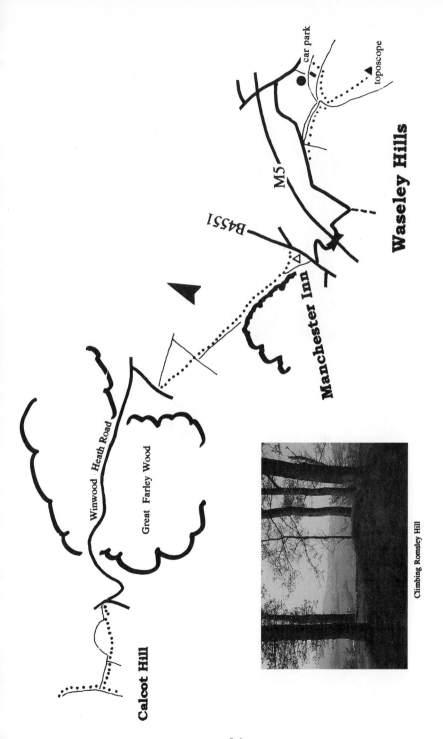

Calcot Hill

Winwood Heath Road

Great Farley Wood

Manchester Inn

B4551

M5

Waseley Hills

car park

toposcope

Climbing Romsley Hill

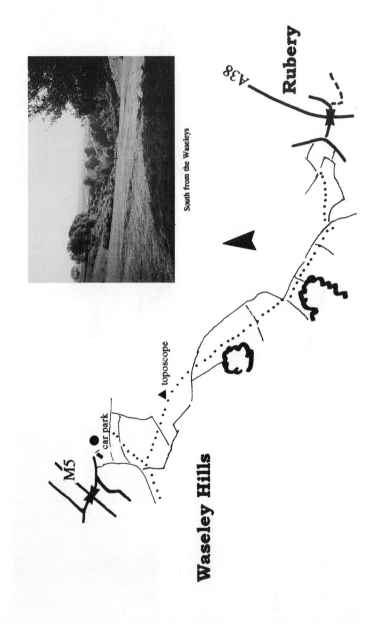

South from the Waseleys

Rubery

A38

toposcope

car park

M5

Waseley Hills

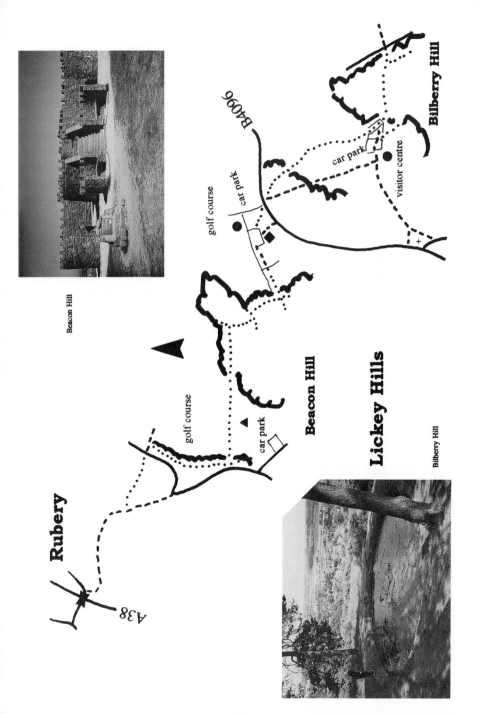

Beacon Hill

B4096

golf course

car park

car park

visitor centre

Bilberry Hill

golf course

car park

Beacon Hill

Lickey Hills

Bilberry Hill

Rubery

A38

36

The **Lickey Hills** covers 526 acres of dramatically rounded heathery hills. Rednall Hill (268 metres) and Beacon Hill (298 metres) sit on the north side of deep, wooded valley, with Bilberry Hill (270 metres) and Cofton Hill (263 metres) to the south. The views are not as wide as from the Waseley or Clent Hills but you can see far over Birmingham. From Bilberry Hill the views are framed with Scots pine and there are distant glimpses of the Bitell Reservoirs.

Call at the Visitor Centre for booklets and leaflets about the complicated geology and history of this area. You will learn about the Stone Age flint, the Roman road, the Royal Hunting forest, the quarries, the beacons and the Devil's Huntsman - who rushes madly about on stormy nights.

The Clent, Waseley and Lickey Hills form a chain of high ground where many small **streams** rise. They travel to all three of our major Midland rivers, the Trent, Severn and Avon, the first joining the North Sea and the others combining at Tewksbury to flow into the Bristol Channel. From the northern flank of the Clent Hills the River Stour runs through the Black Country to join the River Severn, and the Bourne Brook flows east into Birmingham to join the River Rea. The Rea rises on the Lickey Hills and joins the Tame at Spaghetti Junction, which heads for the River Trent. From the southern side of the hills the Battlefield Brook and other streams become the River Salwarpe, which joins the Severn. The Belne Brook collects several small streams and heads south-west for the Severn, while the River Arrow fills the Bitell Reservoirs then runs south into the Avon

The NWP leaves Bilberry Hill through the conifers and crosses green fields on its way to the Bitell Reservoirs. This marks a major change in the character of the walk. From Hagley it has crossed a hilly and dramatic landscape within public parks. The rest of the NWP and the Midland Link follow paths and tracks through a rolling agricultural landscape which is far more typical of the rest of the Midlands.

After a succession of fieldpaths you meet a lane. You may not be conscious of anything momentous as you pass under the railway bridge, but to the south is the infamous **Lickey Bank**. The Birmingham & Gloucester Railway made the unwise decision to build a direct line between Birmingham and Bromsgrove rather than a more easily graded route in the west. The result was the steepest main line gradient in Britain of nearly 2 miles at 1 in 37. This taxed the early engines beyond their powers and the company took the odd step of purchasing some from the USA. They were not so powerful as the makers had promised, the B&G had been done, and trains had to be "banked" by up to four extra locos. The B&G's engineer, Mc Connell, found an answer in a powerful engine of his own design, the secret of which probably was that it worked at a far higher boiler pressure than was considered safe. Mc Connell never revealed the fact. The Midland Railway took over the B&G and in 1924 built *Big Emma*, aka *Big Bertha,* an 0-10-0 of shattering power which saw the line through to almost the end of the steam era. Modern diesels glide up the Lickey Bank with no apparent effort.

St Michael's church is small, secluded and surprisingly rural given that we are not far from Birmingham's southern edge. The original church was built in 1330 but the oldest portions now seem to be the porch and turret from the late 15th century. The rest is Victorian restorative work.

The two **Bitell Reservoirs** were built for the Worcester & Birmingham Canal by damming the River Arrow. More precisely, the canal is supplied with water from the upper lake, which you pass on the NWP. The lower lake gives compensation water for the river to power several local mills. The reservoirs are some of the best places in the Midlands for birds, and particularly duck. You will see mallard, coot and great crested grebe, with moorhens scuttling in the reedy margins near the path. These amiable and familiar creatures would not gain the north edge of the upper reservoir its SSSI status, but a rare plant called mudwort does.

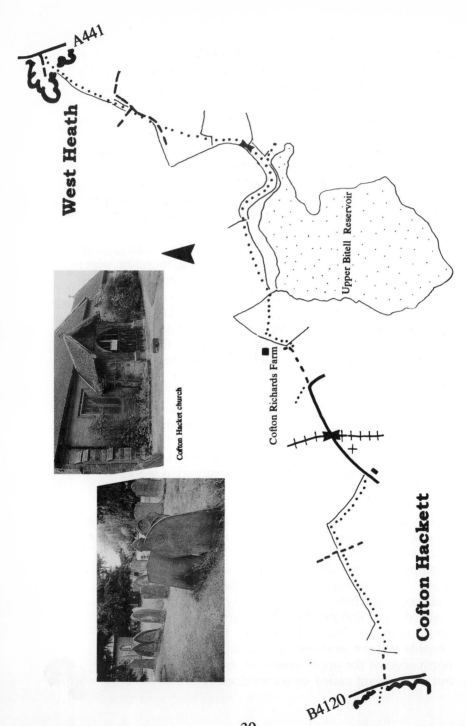

A441

West Heath

Upper Bitell Reservoir

Cofton Hacket church

Cofton Richards Farm

Cofton Hackett

B4120

Rising field paths lead you on to West Heath and the A441. Note the advice I have offered on the map about passing the road junction to minimise contact with traffic. The NWP then takes to the fields again. Quite soon there is a slight rise and the path skirts a deep, wooded hollow. It seems to have been a small quarry and contains a good variety of trees. For the next one third of a mile the NWP follows the edge of playing field owned by Birmingham University. But why do we have to be caged behind 8 stark feet of chain link fence like wild animals? As you reach the lane, note the University's small observatory and their farm opposite.

Far, far underground and running roughly on the line of the lane is the 1.5 mile long **Wast Hill** (or King's Norton) Tunnel. The tunnel and the flight of 30 locks at Tardebigge made the Worcester & Birmingham an expensive canal to build; the landscape mocking the canal as it mocked the railway. There is no towpath so the horses were led across the hill while the boats where legged through, the boatmen lying on their backs and walking their feet along the tunnel walls.

You were rising slightly from the reservoirs, at about 152 metres, to the A441 at 200 metres, and in spite of its name Wast Hill is only 10 metres higher. The ground falls again to 200 metres at Forhill and this is the only ground above 200 metres on the rest of the NWP or the Midland Link.

There is not a lot to tell about the rest of the way to Forhill except that there is a small wood of Scots pines and a deep hollow with a richly overgrown pond, presumably another quarry. But for some reason this quite place stays warmly in the mind as somewhere you would like to go back to.

Forhill has the agreeable Peacock Inn presiding over the junction of a minor rural road with two lanes, and a picnic site. The lane which passes the front of the pub and plunges down the hillside as a track is the Roman road, **Ryknild Street**.

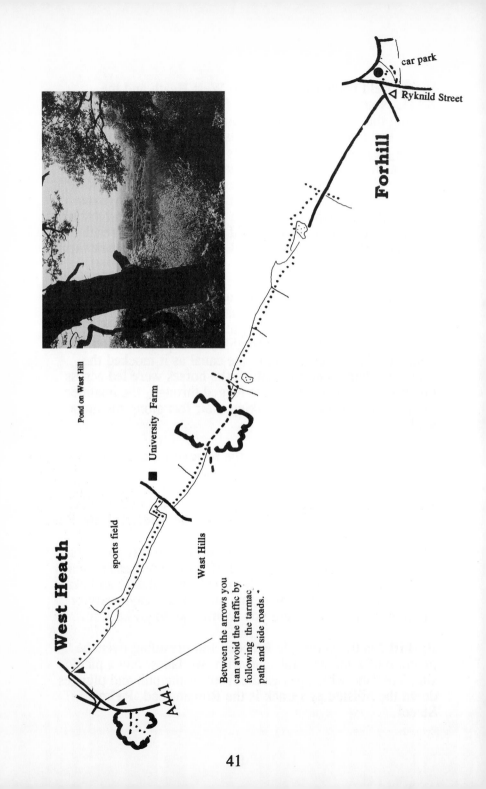

car park

◁ Ryknild Street

Forhill

Pond on West Hill

■ University Farm

sports field

West Hills

West Heath

A441

Between the arrows you
can avoid the traffic by
following the tarmac
path and side roads.

41

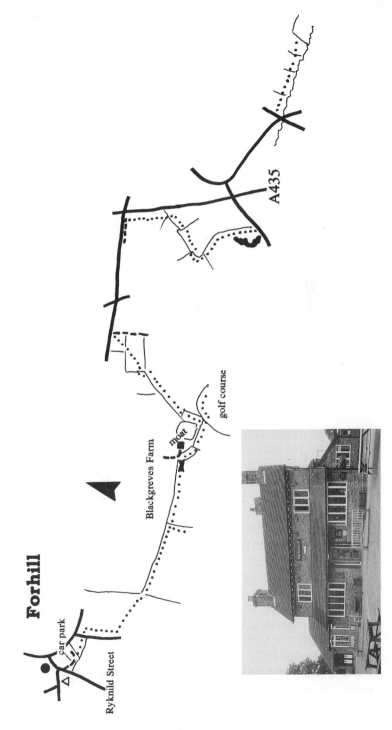

Forhill

Rykmild Street

car park

Blackgreves Farm

moat

golf course

A435

Ryknild Street is shown on the maps. To the north it gets lost in the streets of Birmingham, though we have some Iknield Streets which is an alternative version of the name. To the south, long straight stretches of minor road reach through Beoley, Redditch and Studley, down the A435 through Alcester, crossing the River Avon at Bidford on Avon, then across miles of flat plain through Honeybourne to Weston Subedge and Bourton on the Water. This was an important Roman camp on the Fosse Way, the main route between Lincoln and Exeter. Ryknild Street was the way north to Wall on that other main highway, Watling Street, or our A5. The Romans were not very interested in Birmingham but there was a camp at Metchley, Harborne.

Blackgreaves Farm stands on an island surrounded by a fully watered moat. The present house was built in the early 17th century, but the moat suggests that it replaced an earlier building. By this time in our history, the reign of James I, people had long built houses rather than castles and saw no great need for expensive fortifications. Our most famous Midland moated house is Baddesley Clinton (on the Midland Link), where the original house was 13th century.

The NWP wanders on through fields and along lanes. It is all pleasant and rather unremarkable, without hills or ruins or lakes, until you reach **Berry Mound**. Strictly speaking, you do not reach it, because it is a few yards off route and there is no public access. However, you can see the great ring of trees marking double ramparts which enclose 4.5 hectares. They are now rather breached and worn down, but in the Iron Age period (600BC to 43AD) they must have been formidable. The Mound stands on quite level ground, not a place that a military commander would naturally choose as a stronghold, though it is surrounded on three sides by the River Cole. There is some doubt whether these Iron Age structures were permanently occupied or just safe retreats for local people in times of danger. The encled areas are usually large enough to keep some stock and build houses and this one had a good water supply, unlike many on hilltops.

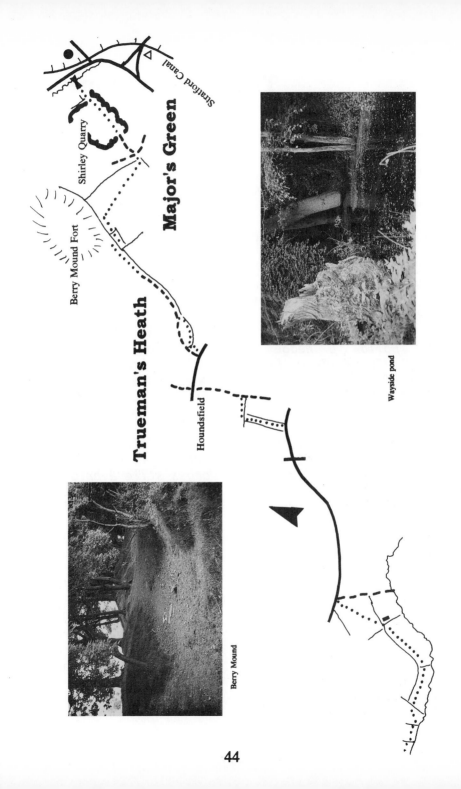

Major's Green

Stratford Canal

Shirley Quarry

Berry Mound Fort

Trueman's Heath

Houndsfield

Wayside pond

Berry Mound

The Midland Link

Forhill

(E1) From picnic site WCs, cross grass area to far end of site & cross mound, then stile, to lane.

(E2) Cross into woodland. Go R on path 150yds & cross stile L. Bear R & (when in view) go to near end of wooden fence & into next field.

(E3) Follow L hedge .4 mile to 100yds from farm. Bear R to pass dumps on your L, then cross bridge & stile.

(E4) Bear R & cross stile. Follow L hedge & cross stile to golf course.

(E5) Go L around mown area to green (with flag). Take path thro thicket, then follow grass paths to end of concrete track. Go L & follow path by fence 350yds, then half R to fairway. Keep same line across corner of course & take midhedge stile.

(E6) Go L by winding hedge to corner of caravan park. Go L on green track & thro farm to road. ▶ *[Wythall]*

(W58) Go R 50yds & take track L before churchyard. Follow into field then by R hedge to its corner. Go R by caravan park & cross stile to golf course.

*(W59) Go half R to edge of fairway & join grass path. Follow by fence for 350yds to its corner. Go on to start of concrete track. Go R on grass path & follow through thicket to edge of course. Follow R hedge, curving L - **WATCH** for & take hidden stile R.*

(W60) Follow R hedge & cross stile. Bear R to cross stile & bridge. Pass dumps & bear R to join field edge. Follow R hedge .4 mile (via stile) to field corner, & take gap.

(W61) Bear a little R & cross field to take midhedge stile. Go R on wooded path by road to path bend, then L onto road. Cross stile opposite into picnic site.

Forhill

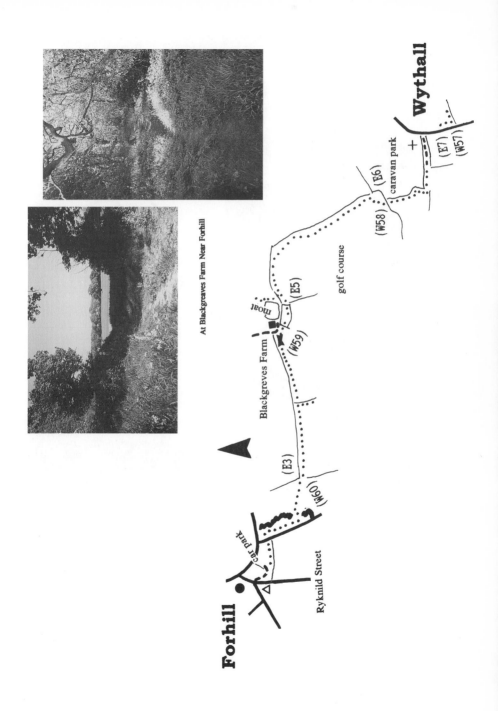

At Blackgreaves Farm Near Forhill

Forhill

car park

Ryknild Street

(W60)

(E3)

Blackgreaves Farm

moat

(W59)

(E5)

golf course

(W58)

(E6)

caravan park

Wythall

(E7)

(W57)

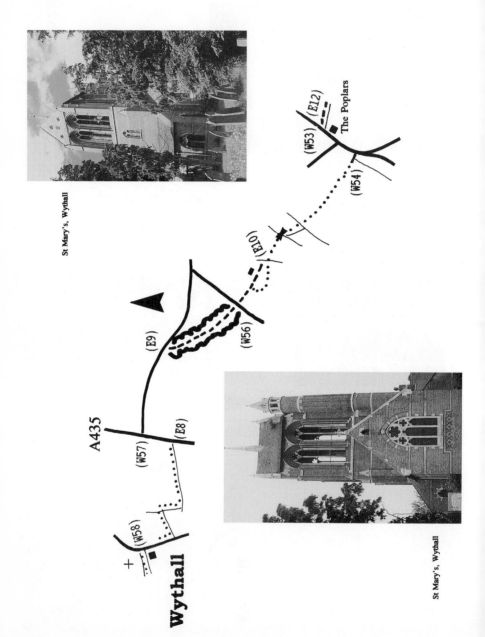

St Mary's, Wythall

The Poplars

(E12)

(W53)

(W54)

(E10)

(E9)

(W56)

A435

(E8)

(W57)

(W58)

Wythall

St Mary's, Wythall

(E)

(E7) Go R 50 yds to timber framed house & cross stile L. Go R & round field corner to next corner, & cross plank. Go R & round field corner to next corner, then cross stile to A435. GREAT CARE.

(E8) Cross, go L 110yds & take lane R. Follow .25 mile & take small gate in fence R.

(E9) Follow woodland track to lane. Take track opposite 100yds to 1st ornamental trees. Go R on grass path thro bushes to cross stile.

(E10) Bear a little R over field to cross bridge & stile. Bear R across field corner & cross stile. Go ahead to chimneys & take gate/stile to road.

(E11) Go L 200yds (past road L) to just past last house R *[Poplars Farm]* & take track R. ➤

(W)

(W53) Go L 200yds (past road R) to L bend, & take gate/stile R.

(W54) Go ahead (sight distant radio mast) & cross stile. Go ahead across field corner to cross stile & bridge.

(W55) Bear a little R over field & cross midhedge stile. Follow grass path thro bushes to drive. Go L to lane.

(W56) Take small gate opposite & follow wooded track to lane. Go L to A435. GREAT CARE.

(W57) Cross & go L 110yds to cross stile R. Follow L hedge round field corner plus 90yds, & cross plank L. Follow L hedge, round field corner plus 100yds & cross stile to road. ◀

From Forhill the Midland Link sets off with the NWP across the fields to Blackgreaves Farm. As the NWP turns north on a woody, wildflowered path, the Link crosses a stile onto a **golf course**. This one is not too bad as golf courses go. You do not have to cross fairways through torrents of balls but amble round the edge. This has been left wild as haven for plants, insects and birds and is free from the manicuring and lawn potions deemed necessary for golf courses.

Conservationists do not like golf courses because they are unatural looking and sterile environments. Fairways are frequently mowed and grow nothing but fine grass, the opposite of the herb rich plant mixture that bugs and birds enjoy. If groundsmen could leave wider and wilder margins to their courses, plant more native species of trees between fairways instead of the ubiquitous Corsican pine, then with some other improved treatment we might end up with golf courses as a better environment than most arable farmland.

The ground slopes slightly to the west and south and the many small ponds on the golf course feed streams which head south-west into the River Arrow, then the Avon. You will shortly leave the Arrow's catchment and start a long, slow descent across the headwaters of the Rivers Cole and Blithe (which join the Tame and Trent) into the valley of the River Avon at Kenilworth.

The new **Britannic Assurance Building** lying next to the golf course is astonishing. The first shock is finding such a thing here at all, when you had thought you were deep in the countryside. The second shock for me is that I find the building rather attractive. A long, spacious, gracious, pavilion, with its flowing roof and cool, watery atmosphere, it seems very sane and businesslike. But should even a good building ever have been permitted on such a rural site?

Forhill is at a height of 200 metres and you are heading towards Earlswood Lakes at about 140 metres. A small rise follows towards Tanworth in Arden and Umberslade Park at 146 metres, but the long fall continues to Kenilworth at 100.

St Mary's church, Wythall was built in 1862 by Preedy, and the tower added in 1903 by W Bidlake. It is in ripe red brick with bands of cream stone edged with blue brick, and the jambs of doors and windows patterned with sawtooth brickwork. The tower is as high Victorian gothic as you get, madly romantic, with those two great openings and their rich shafts, the shadowy lurking bells, the saddleback roof with its fleche in the middle and the secretive polygonal turret running up one corner. From a distance the bell openings look suitably gaunt, ruinous and slightly forbidding. Sadly, St Mary's is in a bad state and not in use.

After an interlude of fieldpaths and a little woodland track the Link arrives at **Clowes Wood.** This wood and the adjoining **New Fallings Coppice** cover 115 acres. Clowes was bought by Warwickshire Wildlife Trust in about 1974 and New Fallings belongs to the Cadbury Trust. Both are open to the public so you can womble about as you please, but don't blame me if you loose the route. Varying levels of soil acidity and boggy areas with pools create different types of habitat. You will find oak and birch woodland, with patches of beech and alder woodland in the low and soggy places. There are areas of bilberry, heather, purple moorgrass and bracken, carpets of bluebell, cow wheat, hairy wood rush and lily of the valley - this is one of its few Warwickshire sites. Wild angelica grows here and there, and wood horsetail thrives in the moist ground.

Earlswood Lakes were built in the late 18th century to feed the Stratford on Avon Canal. The long and surprisingly high dam was built across the north-east side of the valley where several streams gathered to form the River Blythe. Today the Blythe trickles on from an outlet under the centre of the dam. The canal supply runs from a channel at the northern corner. This area is not over endowed with areas of water and the Lakes, along with Bitell Reservoirs, Kingsbury Water Park and Shustoke Reservoirs are precious resources for angling, sailing, getting wet and muddy and their special natural habitat.

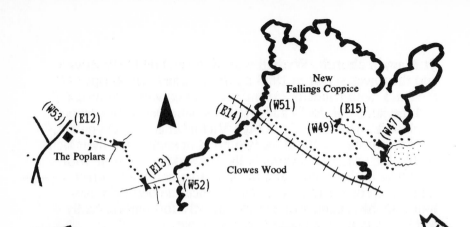

(E12) Follow track to R bend, then go ahead on field edge to cross corner bridge. Go ahead to cross stile & bridge.

(E13) Go L (via gate/ stile) & follow L hedge to cross stile ahead (not L) into wood. Bear L on wood edge path to cross railway footbridge.

(E14) Take path R .4 mile (by railway then curving L) to tiny wooden bridge R. Take path R & cross 2 bridges to track.

(E15) Go R 400yds on winding main track (pass all forks & paths L & R) to a fork with ORANGE MARKER visible 30yds L on wood edge. Take R fork (ignore path R) to twin angled bridges, & cross 1st only. [For a short excursion, see next map.]

(W47) Follow path 33 paces to fork. Go L 25 paces (ignore small path L) to T junction.

(W48) Go L .25 mile on winding main path. Ignore all forks & paths R & some faint ones L, to T junction with 2 plank bridges L.

(W49) Cross plank bridges & follow path 55 paces to T junction at tiny bridge.

(W50) Go L on path .4 mile (curves R & follows railway) to footbridge.

(W51) Cross & go L into wood. Go R on wood edge path to stile & field.

(W52) Go ahead & take gate/stile. Go ahead 20 paces then cross ramp & stile R. Go ahead & cross bridge. Follow L hedge & join track to road.

Earlswood Lakes suffer from algal growth which increases the biochemical oxygen demand of the water. In other words, algae are plants which use up oxygen in the water and do not leave enough for the fish and other water creatures. This is a big problem in most of our lowland lakes and is caused by agricultural nitrate fertilisers which escape and over enrich the water. The quality of the water in the River Blythe is C/C on the Environment Agency scale (which I noted under a comment on the River Stour at the western end of the North Worcs Path) and we can assume the lakes are similar. This is not too good for a river just past its headwaters, the Blythe only starts at The Lakes. Even so, fresh water from several tributaries brings the quality up to C/B when it reaches the River Tame, where it is a very refreshing contribution.

Earlswood Lakes

(E16) Cross bridge R & follow path 100yds then cross bridge R.

(E17) Go L on fenced path & take small gate to Tane. Follow to road. Go R to

Earlswood

(E18) Stand on road facing station & go L. Follow 300yds & take drive R to Whitehouse Farm.

(E19) Pass brick house on your L & follow track thro buildings & down field into storage area. Go L to L side of shed, & cross stile.

(E20) Go ahead with hedge on your L & cross 1st & 2nd stiles. Go half R to projecting hedge corner & cross farm track by 2 stiles.

(E21) Go with hedge on your R & cross field corner bridge. Go ahead to cross stile & bridge into hedged area. Go L thro gap to field corner, then with hedge on your R to stile & road.

◄

(W42) Cross stile & follow L hedge to field corner. Bear L to cross bridge & stile. Go ahead & cross bridge, then follow L hedge to track & 2 stiles

(W43) Go half R to field corner & cross stile. Follow R hedge (via stiles) into storage area.

(W44) Exit on track & follow it thro buildings to lane. Go L to railway.

Earlswood

(W45) Stand on road facing station & go R 100yds to take Cloweswood Lane L. Follow to its end & take small gate. Follow fenced path & cross stile R, then bridge.

(W46) Go L 100yds to 2 angled bridges & cross both.

◄

[See the map for a quick whiz around The Lakes and/ or a trip to the Red Lion]

53

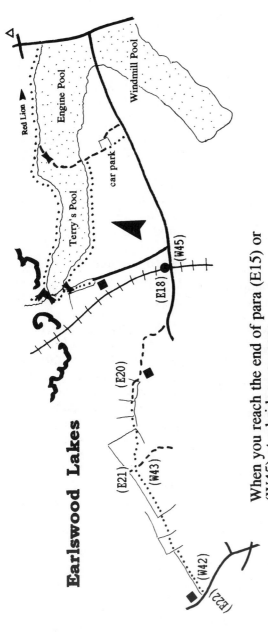

Earlswood Lakes

When you reach the end of para (E15) or (W45) at a bridge you can:

EITHER continue on the main route at paras (E16) or (W46),

OR use the map to walk round The Lakes. Return to the **other** bridge (see map) and resume on para ((E17) or (W47).

54

(E22) Go L .5 mile (over M42 & past 1st house R) to cross stile L near 2nd house.

(E23) Follow R hedge & cross stile R. Follow L hedge & cross stile. Bear L past white house & cross corner stile to reach lane

(E24) Go R .5 mile to B4101 by Old Royal Oak.

(E25) Take track opposite & join woodland path to its end, then cross stile.

(E26) Bear R to three quarters down R hedge, take gate & cross railway.

(E27) Go L to field corner & cross bridge/stile. Follow R hedge (via stile) to cross corner stile by pond. Follow L hedge & join hedged/fenced path to lane. Go L 400yds to War Memorial.

Tanworth in Arden

(E28) From War Memorial pass church on your R & follow road to Butts Lane & grass triangle.

(E29) Go ahead across triangle & take drive to Children's Farm. Follow 1.25 miles (becomes track) to road. ▶

(W35) Go up L past Butts Lane & church to War Memorial.

Tanworth in Arden

(W36) At War Memorial, put Post Office on your R. Go ahead 350yds & pass Bell-field R, plus 50yds, to drive of Little Court.

(W37) Take fenced path on its R & cross stile to field. Follow R hedge to pond & cross stile. Follow L hedge to bottom field corner & cross stile & bridge.

(W38) Go ahead by oaks, then L by hedge to gate R, & cross railway. Go L to top field corner & cross stile. Follow woodland track to B4101 at Old Royal Oak pub.

(W39) Take lane R of pub .5 mile (over railway & past white house R) to white garage L, & cross stile L.

(W40) Go R & cross stile under oak. Go ahead & cross stile. Go L by hedge & cross stile to lane.

(W41) Go R .5 mile (over M42) to 25yds before 1st house R, & take path R. ◀

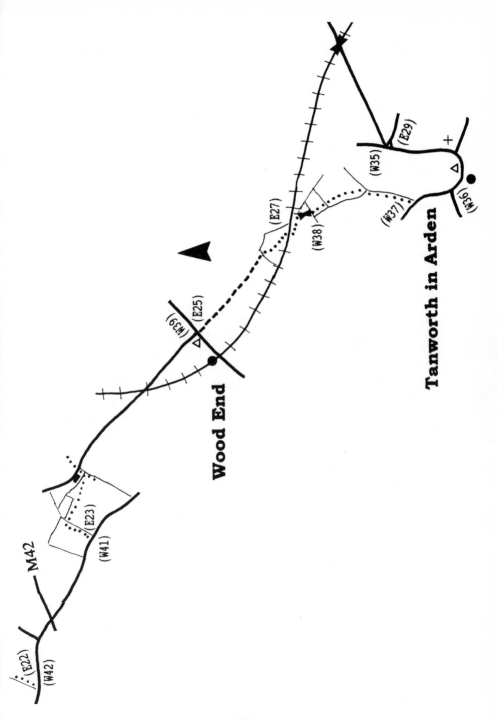

M42

(W42) (E22)

(W41)

(E23)

Wood End

(W39) (E25)

(E27)

(W38)

Tanworth in Arden

(W35) (E29)

(W37)

(W36)

Tanworth in Arden is one of those magical English names and whispers of something between Eden and Arcadia. The buildings are of all heights and shapes and jumble happily along the curved main street. There is one timber framed cottage, but this is a village of Midlands red brick with some fronts washed in white, red or cream. A few houses date from the late 18th century and some are modern, but most are Victorian. The names of The Doctor's House, The Old Boot Shop, the Bankhouse and others tell their story. There is a wine shop, a pub, a post office, a general store and a school.

The church of **St Mary Magdalene** was built mostly between 1300 and 1330 in soft, grey local limestone, but like most churches, it has much Victorian restoration. The mighty square tower has rather a stumpy spire. The interior is large and open with a great deal of good Victorian stained glass. Look for the small window of 1843 on the south wall at the west end which has a range of soft colours, and the simpler design of the 1947 window at the front of the north aisle. The chancel floor has super encaustic floor tiles, the whacking great organ has an ornamental gothic case, there is an 18th century font, an 8 foot long wooden chest from the 13th century, and a lectern eagle checking that everyone is paying attention. Get the leaflet and leave plenty of money to keep it all going.

Umberslade Children's Farm is just off route on the way to Umberslade Hall. It offers to children "listening, feeling and smelling" animals as part of the farm experience, and perhaps to some grown ups who secretly fancy some piglet cuddling.

The long, rising wooded track was once the **carriage drive** to Umberslade Hall. The lower section has been surfaced and is lined with immense poplars, but the track which continues was lined with elms which perished from Dutch Elm Disease. The result is a jungle of mainly shrubby elm growing from the roots of dead parents.

Umberslade Hall was described by Horace Walpole in 1751 as "an odious place". At that time it was a single stone block nine bays long with the central five slightly recessed. Since then a colonnade, a pillared porch and wings have been added. It is difficult to see much of it but I am not sure that Walpole would now think differently. The house has been broken up into luxury flats.

Across the M42 you finally meet the **obelisk** which was erected in 1749 by Thomas Archer, probably to mark his getting a peerage. Obelisks are intended to impress by being glimpsed from a distance, and this one must intrigue millions who travel the M42. Close to, it is rather weedy and much less imposing, rather like the experience of actually meeting someone famous.

Tanworth in Arden

58

Nuthurst

(E33)

(W30)

(W31)

obelisk

(E32)

M40

(W33)

Umberslade Hall

(E31)

(E30)

(W34)

(E29)

(W35)

E

W

(E30) Go R 150yds to corner of wood L. Take path L to iron kissing gate & field.

(E31) Follow L fence .35 mile (via small gate) till fence bends L. Bear R (via iron gate, stile & projecting fence corner) to M40 tunnel.

(E32) Follow lane to T junction. Go R to farm L & cross stile R. Bear L to R end of brick shed & take gate/stile. Go to bottom L field corner & cross bridge to green track.

(W30) Take green track opposite 100yds to cross bridge & stile R. Head for L end of brick shed & take gate/stile. Head for R end of grey roof & cross stile to lane.

(W31) Go L to bottom. Take gate/stile L & follow lane under M40 to field.

(W32) LOOK PAST MIDFIELD POWER POLE & head for stile. Go R via small iron gate to meet fence.

(W33) Go L by fence (via small gates) & join fenced path to road.

(W34) Go R 150yds & take track L. Follow 1.25 mile (becomes drive) to lane.

59

Lapworth's church of St Mary the Virgin is a powerful little huddle of grey limestone. There are traces of 12th century work in the nave but it has been extended and improved over the centuries. The tower is detached and is in the Decorated style, but the overall impression of the church comes from the square headed windows in the clerestory roof which are of the later, Perpendicular, period, ie late 14th to mid 16th centuries.

From Forhill to the railway station at Wood End the landscape has been pretty level with just a gradual fall. From here through Tanworth, Umberslade Park and Lapworth all the way to Baddesley Clinton are green rises and folds. It is not so dramatic as most of the North Worcs Path, but makes a very attractive and satisfying walk.

St Mary the Virgin, Lapworth

Heading for Kingswood

60

(E33) Go L to lane. Cross stile opposite & follow L hedge to cross top corner stile. Cross field diagonally to stile & drive.

(E34) Go L 250yds to 12yds before speed bump, & cross stile R. Go half L past shed to gravel drive. Go R a few paces & cross stile L. Go half R & cross corner stile. Follow fenced path to A3400.

(E35) Cross & go L a few paces to cross stile. Go to far R field corner. Cross bridge/stile & follow fence to lane.

(E36) Go R 60yds & take small gate L. Go half R past projecting fence corner & keep same line to midhedge gate. DON'T TAKE IT. Go R down field edge & take small corner gate.

(E37) Bear R to field bottom gate & cross plank & stile. Head for church (via gate) & cross stile to lane. *(Lapworth)*

(E38) Go R a few paces, enter churchyard, & follow stone path to lane. Cross stile opposite & go parallel with L hedge to cross midhedge stile. ▶

(W24) Bear R a few paces & cross stile. Go ahead & take gate. Keep same line over crest to gate, & cross stile & plank.

(W25) Go ahead to projecting hedge corner & take small gate. Go R by hedge to gate R. DON'T TAKE IT. Go half L past projecting fence corner & keep same line to small midhedge & lane.

(W26) Go R 60yds to drive & take path L by fence. Follow fence to cross bridge & stile. Go L to far hedge & cross midhedge stile to A3400.

(W27) Go L a few paces, (GREAT CARE) cross road to electrical gizmo & take stile. Follow fenced path & cross stile.

(W28) Go half R & cross midfence stile to drive. Go R to end of tarmac & turn L past shed, then bear R to stile & drive.

(W29) Go L to end of tarmac & cross stile R. Cross field diagonally & take stile. Go to bottom R corner & cross stile to lane. ◀

E

(E39) Go half R to far end of pond, then R to cross stile. Go ahead & pass deep deep hollow on your R, then parallel with R hedge to cross midhedge stile.◄

(E40) Go ahead & cross stile to cricket ground. Head just R of pavilion & take SMALL gate

(E41) Follow R hedge (via dip & past gate R) to L of steel gates, & cross stile onto road. Go L to canal & join towpath. ►

Stratford Canal

(E42)

Lapworth

Nuthurst

Nuthurst Grange

A3400

W

(W21) Follow L hedge (past gate L & across dip) & take small corner gate to cricket field.

(W22) Head 20yds L of score board & cross stile. Go ahead & cross stile. Keep parallel with L hedge pass hollow L to field corner, & cross stile.►

(W23) ► Pass end of pond & go half L to cross mid-hedge stile. Go ahead to far R field corner & cross stile to lane. Cross to R of wide gateway & take small gates, then pass church to lane.

62

(E42) Go R 1.2 miles to finger post by footbridge at canal junction.

Kingswood

(E43) From finger post by footbridge at canal junction, pass cottage on your R, cross bridge & follow towpath 250yds to brick bridge & Grand Union Canal. Go L over bridge, follow towpath to 1st bridge & rise to road. GREAT CARE - DO NOT CROSS.

(E44) Go R on verge 200yds to Manor House gate R.

(E45) GREAT CARE. Cross & take track to its end, & cross stile to yard. Cross yard & take stile R of brick shed. Cross field diagonally & take corner stile.

(E46) Follow R hedge .3 mile (via stile) to hedge corner. Keep same line & cross stile onto drive.

(E47) Go R (on L fork), pass car park & take path L. Pass church & take gate to track. Follow (via gate) to lane.

(W15) Follow track to lane. Go L 40yds & take track R. Follow (via gates) to pass church & join path to its end. Go R past car park to fork of drive.

(W16) Cross stile L. **LOOK AT HOUSE** then wood on its R, & aim for wood's R end. Go with fence/hedge on your L .3 mile (via stiles) to field with pylon & red shed.

(W17) Cross diagonally to L end of shed & cross stile to yard. Go ahead & cross stile, then follow track to B4439.

(W18) GREAT CARE - CROSS ROAD HERE. Go R on verge 200yds & cross bridge. Take steps L to towpath.

(W19) Go ahead to canal junction & turn R. Go 200yds to lock, cross bridge & follow towpath to finger post.

Kingswood

(W20) From canal junction by finger post head for "Kings Norton". Follow towpath .8 mile to Bridge 32 by cottage. Cross canal & go on to Bridge 31. Exit L, go to end of R hedge & cross stile R.

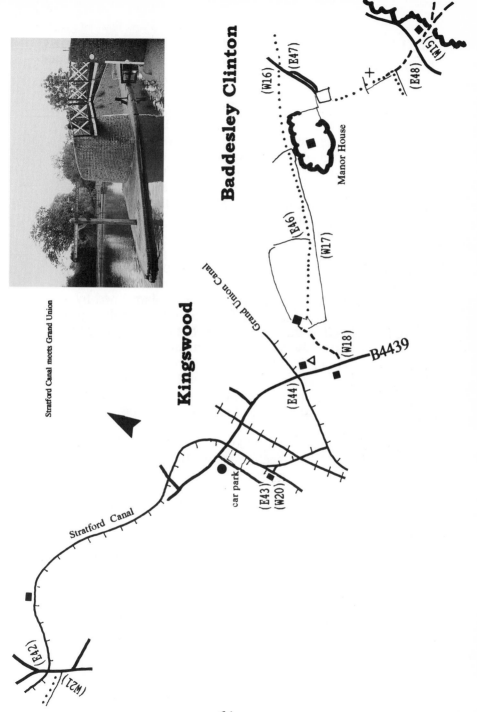

Stratford Canal meets Grand Union

Baddesley Clinton

(W15)

(E47)

(W16)

(E48)

Manor House

(E46)

(W17)

Kingswood

Grand Union Canal

(W18)

B4439

(E44)

car park

(E43)
(W20)

Stratford Canal

(E42)

(W21)

The Link soon joins the Stratford on Avon Canal and follows
a flight of locks down to **Kingswood Junction,** where a spur
links it to the Grand Union Canal.

The **Stratford Canal** starts at Kings Norton in Birmingham
where it leaves the Worcester & Birmingham Canal. There
are 55 locks in its meandering 25 miles, white drawbridges
and strange barrel roofed cottages. Like the Staffs & Worcs
Canal, the Stratford is a contour canal which follows the
lie of the land. The northern section between Kings Norton
and Kingswood was opened in 1803, but the southern part
was not completed until 1815.

The Stratford was suffering from railway competition in
1835, but its decline was long, slow and painful. The odd
working boat still used the northern section in the 1950s.
The southern section had been pretty well abandoned by
the 1930s. Closure of the Stratford and other canals was
being considered in the early 1950s, but the cost of getting
rid of any canal is shocking, almost always more than the
cost of maintaining it. This cheerful bit of economics and
a massive public campaign resulted in the 1959 decision to
keep the Stratford open. The southern section was taken
over by the National Trust and reopened in 1964.

The **Grand Union** links London with Leicester, Nottingham
and Birmingham. This section leaves Birmingham via Small
Heath and Hay Mills and runs through Solihull. After Kingswood Junction it heads down the Hatton Locks to Warwick.
This canal is one of the second generation which were built
in direct lines to cut travelling time. The pounds are long
and straight, there are deep flights of locks, mighty cuttings
and lofty embankments. In the 1930s the Government spent
much money in improving the GU as a working canal. This
did not succeed in reviving its trade, but the GU was never
in such a state as the Stratford or threatened with closure.

At Baddesley Clinton you meet the **Heart of England Way**
on its 100 mile route between Cannock Chase and Bourton
on the Water in the Cotswolds. At Kenilworth you meet the
Centenary Way. The Midland Link and the North Worcs
Path run to Kinver Edge and complete a circle round the
West Midlands area close to 100 miles.

Baddesley Clinton Manor is one of the few perfect media-
eval manor houses, surrounded by a moat with the entrance
guarded by a crenellated gatehouse. The first manor was
built in the 13th century but most of the present building
is from the 15th and 16th. For some 500 years it belonged
to the Roman Catholic Ferrers family until it came to the
National Trust in 1940. The house is, of course, haunted.
There is a priest who takes his kit out of one box and puts
it into another, a mysterious lady sitting in the library,
footsteps that try door handles, an army officer, rapping
and cloth tearing noises and a dishy young lady in black.

St Michael's church at Baddesley Clinton is quite small.
It has a Perpendicular tower and part of the nave is 13th
century, but it has been much added to and altered and the
whole lot was restored by the Victorians. There is a fine
chancel screen and a unique Sarah Green chamber organ.

Hay Wood covers 200 acres and is said to be one of the
remaining fragments of the Forest of Arden. Since it is
shrouded in dark conifers this seems surprising, but Hay
Wood is "ancient woodland". This means that it has been
woodland under trees of some sort since the 1600s, and
may therefore have been in this state much longer, even
since the last ice melted some 10,000 years ago. Today
though, Hay Wood's main purpose is timber production.
The wide forest rides are pleasant walks, if not especially
interesting. However, there are bright flowers such as
trailing yellow pimpernel, and I recently met here the
local recorder of Butterfly Conservation who was out
looking for a variety of white butterfly.

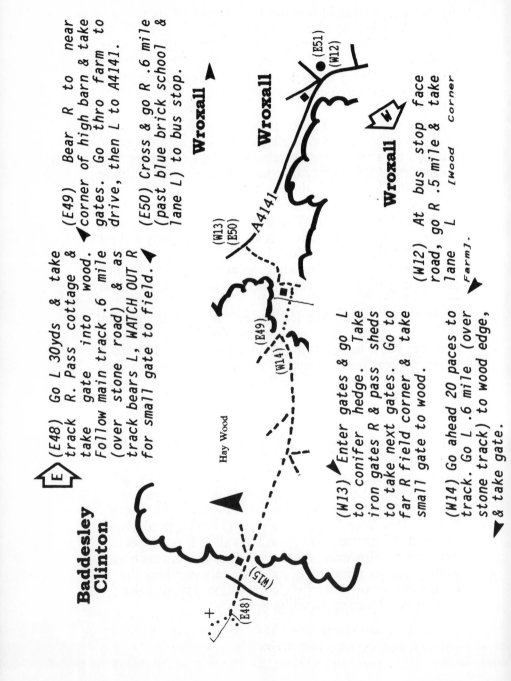

Baddesley Clinton

(E48) Go L 30yds & take track R. Pass cottage & take gate into wood. Follow main track .6 mile (over stone road) & as track bears L, WATCH OUT R for small gate to field.

(E49) Bear R to near corner of high barn & take gates. Go thro farm to drive, then L to A4141.

(E50) Cross & go R .6 mile (past blue brick school & lane L) to bus stop.

(W13) Enter gates & go L to conifer hedge. Take iron gates R & pass sheds to take next gates. Go to far R field corner & take small gate to wood.

(W14) Go ahead 20 paces to track. Go L .6 mile (over stone track) to wood edge, & take gate.

(W12) At bus stop face road, go R .5 mile & take lane L [Wood Corner Farm].

Hay Wood

Wroxall

Wroxall

Wroxall

A4141

(W13)
(E50)

(E49)

(W14)

(E51)
(W12)

(STM)

(E48)

67

Wroxall School (now a nursery) and the nearby houses are similar in style because they were all part of the Wroxall Abbey estate. The Abbey is out of sight, which is probably just as well because Pevsner describes it as "large and high and rather joyless". But the school is very jolly, with zizzy red and white bands and window arches against blue brick.

Kenilworth Castle marks the end of the Midland Link, but this although last stretch is across the flatest landscape on the Link or the NWP, you can't see the castle for any great distance. It does stand on a slight rise, but its defences on this (east) side depended on a lake, long since drained.

The Castle was started in 1120 when Henry I gave it to Geoffrey de Clinton. In 1173 Henry II obliged Henry de Clinton to swop it for other land and Kenilworth became a Royal castle. King John was a frequent visitor and may have enlarged the dam to raise the level of the lake. Kenilworth was one of the Royal castles to be surrendered to the Barons after the signing of Magna Carta, but seems never to have been handed over.

This was was where Simon de Montfort held Prince Edward hostage against his father, Henry III. However Edward got away and raised an army which attacked a force under de Montfort's son, Simon, camped near the castle. Simon escaped by swimming the moat in his night clothes. Following de Montfort's defeat at the Battle of Evesham, the garrison refused to surrender. Henry and Edward blockaded the castle and attacked by mining it, by trying to scale the walls and to cross the lake on boats brought from Chester. Only after a year at the end of 1266 did the rebels run short of food and ammunition to surrender on good terms.

Kenilworth saw spectacular tournaments, the abdication of Edward II and three visits by Queen Elizabeth I. The castle was garrisoned by Parliament during the Civil War but not attacked. It was sleighted in 1649 to neuralise its military strength and the lake was drained.

(E51) At bus stop face road, go L 150yds & take 1st lane L. Follow .4 mile to A4117.

(E52) Cross into lane opposite & go 100yds to crossroads. Go R 150yds & cross stile L.

(E53) Go half R to bottom field corner & cross footbridge. Go ahead by R hedge & through wide hedge gap to corner of next field.

(E54) Go half R to field bottom (head 20yds L of power pole near conifers) & cross stile. Go ahead & cross stile. Follow green track, then lane, to road.

(E55) Take lane opposite [Barracks Lane] to its end, & follow path to stile & field. Go ahead to last oak & cross stile.

(E56) Go ahead parallel with L hedge to lone tree & cross stile to lane. Take track opposite to sharp L bend & cross stile ahead.

(E57) Go parallel with L hedge (over brook) to lone tree, & cross stile. Go ahead on same line to cross next stile. ➤

(W5) Go ahead & cross stile. Bear R to lone tree & cross stile. Go parallel with R hedge & cross brook. Ignore path bearing L & go on to gate/stile & track.

(W6) Follow to lane. Cross stile opposite & go parallel with R hedge to cross stile.

(W7) Go ahead with oaks on your L (REPEAT - L) & cross stile. Follow path, then drive, to road.

(W8) Take lane opposite [Butlers End], then green lane, & cross stile. Go ahead to cross field bottom stile.

(W9) Go to top R field corner, then R by line of oaks to cross footbridge. Go half L to 20yds L of power pole with gizmo, & cross stile to road.

(W10) Go R 150yds to crossroads. Go L to end of lane & (CAREFUL) cross A4117 into lane opposite.

(W11) Go .4 mile to A4141. Go R 150yds to bus stop.

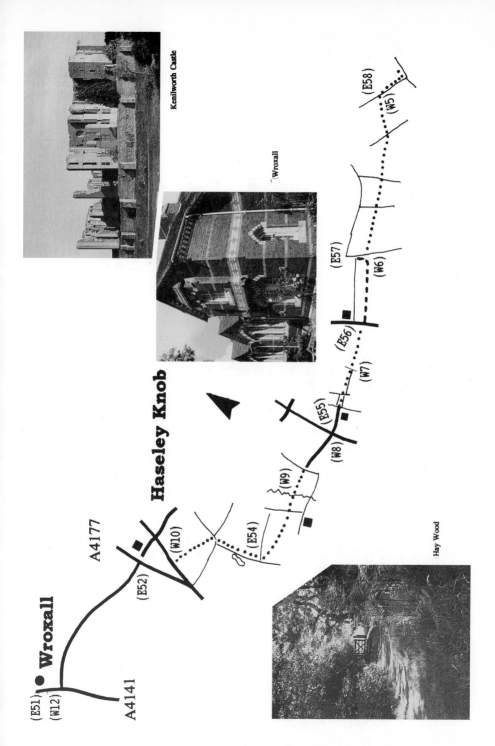

Kenilworth Castle

Wroxall

Haseley Knob

Wroxall

A4177

A4141

Hay Wood

(E51)
(W12)

(E52)

(W10)

(E54)

(W9)

(W8)

(E55)

(W7)

(E56)

(E57)

(W6)

(E58)

(W5)

70

Kenilworth

(E58) Go R by hedge & round field corner. Follow R hedge .25 mile, pass pond & go round corner to take gateway R.

(E59) Head 100yds R of L field corner & cross stile. Keep same line to lone tree & cross stile.

(E60) Keep same line (via stile) to cross footbridge. Go half L towards power pole & cross hedge corner stile.

(E61) Follow R hedge (via stiles) & cross corner stile to car park.

Kenilworth

(W1) At car park on S side of castle, face castle, go L to notice board & cross stile.

(W2) Go L by hedge .6 mile (via stiles), & after power lines cross next corner stile to field.

(W3) SIGHT 3rd pylon from L, cross to it & take footbridge & stile. Keep same line (via stile) to cross stile near pylon.

(W4) Go to far R field corner & take gateway. Go L past pond & follow L hedge .25 mile (through hedge gap & past end of track L) to next field corner. Go R by hedge 150yds & cross stile L.

castle

car park

(E61)

(W3)

(E60)

(W4)

(E59)

(E58)

(W5)

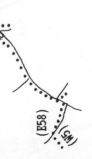

71

Qu*ercus

... publishing interesting books ...

QuercuS is a regional publisher specialising in books about the Midlands, with some on Wales. Phone, fax or write for a full catalogue.

Wales
The Trackway of the Cross (£3.50)
Australian Williams (£3.50)

History
Midland Castles (£7.50)
Historic Houses & Gardens (£7.50)
Coaching Days in the Midlands (£7.50)

Pen & Ink Sketch Albums
Sketches of Hales Owen (£7.50)
Sketches of Hales Owen II (£7.50)
Sketches of Birmingham (£7.50)
Sketches of Bromsgrove (£7.50)

Natural History
Midland Woods & Forests (7.95)
Midland Rivers (£7.95)

Mysterious Midlands
Midland Ghosts & Hauntings (£6.95)
Midland Spirits & Spectres (£7.50)
Midland Murders & Mysteries (£7.50)

Lives
Us Kids (£7.50)
Heart in my Boots (£3.95)

67 Cliffe Way, Warwick CV34 5JG
01926 776363

outdoor stuff

Long Distance Routes
Step by step guides in both directions.

Heart of England Way (£6.45)
Warwickshire's Centenary Way (£6.45)
Birmingham to Aberystwyth Walk (1999)
Llangollen to Caernarfon Walk (1999)
Birmingham to Bala Walk (some time)

DaywalkS Footpath Networks
Networks of linked paths in rather special areas.

Cannock Chase (£4.95)
Vale of Llangollen (£4.95)
Wyre Forest (£4.95)

Strolls & Walks
A easy stroll and a longer walk from nice places.

Strolls & Walks from Picnic Places (Midlands) (£4.95)
Strolls & Walks from Cotswold Villages (£4.95)
Strolls & Walks from Midland Villages (£5.50)

Walks around...
Local walks for residents and visitors.

Twenty Walks around Rugby (£4.95)
Ten Walks around Coventry (£3.75)
Twenty Walks around Stourbridge (£4.75)

*
WALKWAYS

67 Cliffe Way, Warwick CV34 5JG
01926 776363

JOIN THE

Worcestershire Wildlife Trust

We have already:
- **established 70 nature reserves**
- **encouraged the return of the otters**
- **gained a reputation second to none**

We need:
- **more members**
- **more money**
- **more volunteers**

SEND A DONATION OR BECOME A MEMBER
I would like to become a member £22 per annum
Return with payment (cheques payable to
Worcestershire Wildlife Trust)

Please send me more details about the Trust

I would like to make a donation

Worcestershire Wildlife Trust
FREEPOST (WR28) Worcester WR5 7BR
Tel: 01905 754919

Dry beech woodland and
lush undergrowth show the
contrasts in Clowes Wood
(page 50)